A Visit to the City

Mary Rose

T0346720

Name _____

Age _____

Class _____

OXFORD
UNIVERSITY PRESS

OXFORD
UNIVERSITY PRESS

Great Clarendon Street, Oxford OX2 6DP

Oxford University Press is a department of the University of Oxford.
It furthers the University's objective of excellence in research, scholarship,
and education by publishing worldwide in

Oxford New York

Auckland Cape Town Dar es Salaam Hong Kong Karachi
Kuala Lumpur Madrid Melbourne Mexico City Nairobi
New Delhi Shanghai Taipei Toronto

With offices in

Argentina Austria Brazil Chile Czech Republic France Greece
Guatemala Hungary Italy Japan South Korea Poland Portugal
Singapore Switzerland Thailand Turkey Ukraine Vietnam

OXFORD and OXFORD ENGLISH are registered trade marks of
Oxford University Press in the UK and in certain other countries

ISBN-13: 978 0 19 440095 4

Printed in China

ACKNOWLEDGEMENTS

The publisher would like to thank the following for their kind permission to reproduce the following:
Alamy Stock Photo pp 4 (train under bridge/Colin Underhill), 4 (tunnel/Martyn
Williams_images), 4 (viaduct/paul weston), 10 (monkeys/Natural Visions), 10 (elephants/
Parmorana), 14 (vintage dress/Heritage Image Partnership Ltd), 14 (car/palle porila),
14 (gallery/Richard Green), 16 (skytrain/mauritius images GmbH), 22 (bridge/Horizon
International Images Limited); OUP p20 (fruit market/Digital Vision); **Shutterstock** pp 2
(train at station/Christian Mueller), 6 (traffic jam/chuyuss), 8 (park/f1 1photo), 10 (giraffes/
Nagel Photography), 10 (panda), 12 (museum/Kamira).
Cover courtesy of Steve Tulley/Alamy Stock Photo
Illustrations by: Mark Ruffle

With thanks to Sally Spray for her contribution to this series

Reading Dolphins
Notes for teachers & parents

Using the book

1 Begin by looking at the first story page (page 2). Look at the picture and ask questions about it. Then read the story text under the picture with your students. **Use section 1 of the CD for this if possible.**

2 Teach and check the understanding of any new vocabulary. Note that some of the words are in the **Picture Dictionary** at the back of the book.

3 Now look at the activities on the right-hand page. Show the example to the students and instruct them to complete the activities. This may be done individually, in pairs, or as a class.

4 Do the same for the remaining pages of the book.

5 Retell the whole story more quickly, reinforcing the new vocabulary. **Sections 2 and 3 of the CD can help with this.**

6 **If possible, listen to the expanded story (section 4 of the CD). The students should follow in their books.**

7 When the book is finished, use the **Picture Dictionary** to check that students understand and remember new vocabulary. **Section 5 of the CD can help with this.**

Using the CD

The CD contains five sections.

1 The story told slowly, with pauses. Use this during the first reading. It may also be used for "Listen and repeat" activities at any point.

2 The story told at normal speed. This should be used once the students have read the book for the first time.

3 The story chanted. Students may want to chant along with the story.

4 The expanded story. The story is told in a longer version. This will help the students understand English when it is spoken faster, as they will now know the story and the vocabulary.

5 Vocabulary. Each word in the **Picture Dictionary** is spoken and then used in a simple sentence.

Today is a holiday.
Let's go to the city.
Come on, get on the train.
We are going to the city.

Trace and connect.

taxi

car

train

plane

bicycle

motorcycle

boat

bus

Look. The train is going under a bridge, into a tunnel, and over a river.

Look and write.

❶ The car is going
<u>under</u> a bridge.

❷ The bus is going
_____ a tunnel.

❸ The plane is going
_____ a river.

❹ The bicycle is going
_____ a bridge.

❺ The motorcycle is going
_____ a tunnel.

❻ The taxi is going
_____ a bridge.

Here we are. We are in the city. Look at the busy street and all the cars. There are so many.

Circle yes **or** no .

❶ There are taxis.
yes
no

❷ The taxis are red.
yes
no

❸ There are tall buildings.
yes
no

❹ There is a train.
yes
no

❺ There is a bicycle.
yes
no

❻ There is a plane.
yes
no

❼ There is a river.
yes
no

❽ There is a tunnel.
yes
no

Let's go to the park.
There are many things to see.
There is a lake, and there are boats on the lake.

Read and circle.

❶ There **(is)** / are a boat.

❷ There is / are a lake.

❸ There is / are boats on the lake.

❹ There is / are people in the boats.

❺ There is / are tall buildings.

❻ There is / are a tall white building.

❼ There is / are trees.

❽ There is / are a red tree.

Look at the animals.
There's a zoo in the park.
There are giraffes, elephants,
monkeys, and a panda.

Circle.

❶ Monkeys are **(smart)** / stupid .

❷ Giraffes are **tall** / short .

❸ Pandas are black and **red** / white .

❹ Elephants are **small** / big .

❺ An elephant's nose is **long** / short .

❻ Pandas are **thin** / fat .

❼ Elephants are **weak** / strong .

❽ A giraffe's neck is **long** / short .

There is a big new museum
in the city. There are many
old things in the museum.
Let's go and see.

The Museum of Inventions.
Read and connect.

train •
(eighteen seventy-six)

1

1888

TV •
(nineteen twenty-three)

2

1876

car •
(eighteen ninety-five)

3

1903

camera •
(eighteen eighty-eight)

4

1923

plane •
(nineteen hundred and three)

5

1895

Look at all these old things.
There is an old car. There is a
long dress. There are some
beautiful pictures, too.

Write There is or There are.

❶ _There_ _is_ a new museum.

❷ _____ _____ old things in the museum.

❸ _____ _____ a long dress.

❹ _____ _____ an old car.

❺ _____ _____ beautiful pictures.

❻ _____ _____ some people in the museum.

❼ _____ _____ three pictures.

❽ _____ _____ two people.

Let's take the skytrain.
This is really cool.
Look down at the street.
The people look so small.

What can you see? Write.

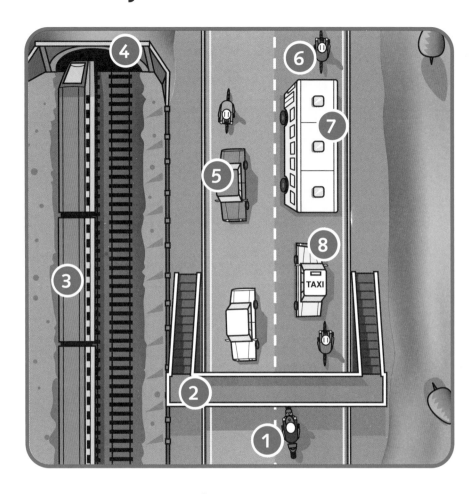

1 motorcycle   **5** _____

2 _____   **6** _____

3 _____   **7** _____

4 _____   **8** _____

We are really high up.
We are at the top of a tall
building. It's a beautiful day.
We can see so far.

Circle yes **or** no .

❶ There is a tunnel.

yes
(no)

❷ There is some water.

yes
no

❸ There are some boats.

yes
no

❹ There is a plane.

yes
no

❺ There are some cars.

yes
no

❻ There are some trees.

yes
no

❼ There is a panda.

yes
no

❽ There are many tall buildings.

yes
no

I'm hungry.
Let's go to the market.
Look at all this fruit.
What fruit do you like?

Trace and connect.

a pineapple   •

a lemon   •

an apple   •

watermelon   •

an orange   •

a banana   •

grapes   •

strawberries   •

1

2

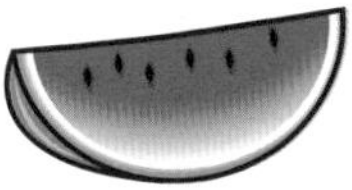

3

4

5

6

7

8

It's seven o'clock.
The sun is going down.
It's time to go home.
What a great day in the city.

Write There is or There are.

1. <u>There</u> <u>are</u> many tall buildings.

2. _____ _____ a park.

3. _____ _____ some trees in the park.

4. _____ _____ a lake in the park.

5. _____ _____ a zoo.

6. _____ _____ many animals in the zoo.

7. _____ _____ a market.

8. _____ _____ a lot of fruit in the market.

Picture Dictionary

bicycle    car

boat    giraffe

bridge    grapes

bus    lemon

motorcycle  strawberries

panda  taxi

pineapple 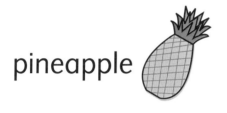 train

plane  tunnel

river  watermelon

Dolphin Readers

Dolphin Readers are available at five levels, from Starter to 4.

The Dolphins series covers four major themes:

Grammar, Living Together, The World Around Us, Science and Nature.

For each theme, there are two titles at every level.

Activity Books are available for all Dolphins.

All Dolphins are available on audio CD.
(2 TITLES ON EACH CD ⊘ SEE TABLE BELOW)

Teacher's Notes are available at **www.oup.com/elt/dolphins**

	Grammar	Living Together	The World Around Us	Science and Nature
Starter	• Silly Squirrel • Monkeying Around ⊘	• My Family • A Day with Baby ⊘	• Doctor, Doctor • Moving House ⊘	• A Game of Shapes • Baby Animals ⊘
Level 1	• Meet Molly • Where Is It? ⊘	• Little Helpers • Jack the Hero ⊘	• On Safari • Lost Kitten ⊘	• Number Magic • How's the Weather? ⊘
Level 2	• Double Trouble • Super Sam ⊘	• Candy for Breakfast • Lost! ⊘	• A Visit to the City • Matt's Mistake ⊘	• Numbers, Numbers Everywhere • Circles and Squares ⊘
Level 3	• Students in Space • What Did You Do Yesterday? ⊘	• New Girl in School • Uncle Jerry's Great Idea ⊘	• Just Like Mine • Wonderful Wild Animals ⊘	• Things That Fly • Let's Go to the Rainforest ⊘
Level 4	• The Tough Task • Yesterday, Today, and Tomorrow ⊘	• We Won the Cup • Up and Down ⊘	• Where People Live • City Girl, Country Boy ⊘	• In the Ocean • Go, Gorillas, Go ⊘